Plant Stories of the Chihuahuan Desert

by Tom Hyden

Illustrations by Lise Spargo

Contents

Introduction

We moved to New Mexico in 1998 and soon after that I began growing vegetables for sale locally. In 2013 I was ready to try something new. Gardening was still appealing to me, but I no longer wanted to grow fragile and human-dependent tomatoes and onions. The Desert Arboretum at Bosque del Apache National Wildlife Refuge (Bosque del Apache) seemed like the perfect place for me.

The National Wildlife Refuge System was created by Congress in the late 1930s with the intent of setting aside unique areas for wildlife protection and creating employment during the Great Depression. (See *Bosque del Apache: A Brief History,* by Robyn Harrison) The Bosque del Apache National Wildlife Refuge was established in 1939, and soon thereafter a Civilian Conservation Corps camp was located there. The young men who served there built the infrastructure of the refuge, including the houses and offices for staff. One of those houses was to become part of the Desert Arboretum. In 1998, refuge staff member Daniel Perry, while living in the house now known as the Friends' House, began building a small cactus garden with the help of part-time refuge employee Socorro Gonzales. In 1999, Percy Deal, a retired hospital administrator, began volunteering at the refuge and was interested in expanding the cactus garden. Refuge Manager Phil Norton agreed to provide rock and gravel and sand if Percy and Socorro would build the garden as we see it today. They constructed hills and paths and planted hundreds of cactus and other desert plants.

Today the Desert Arboretum is still part of the refuge, but the garden itself is managed by the Friends of Bosque del Apache, and the former residence is their headquarters. The Friends exists to support the mission of the refuge through education, funding for research, and activities such as the Festival of the Cranes in November every year.

My first task when I started work in the garden was to do a complete inventory of the surviving plants. Armed with photos, common names and genus/species, I ventured into the Internet to bring our plant list up to date. The following are the stories that I found about the plants in our Desert Arboretum.

What is a Desert?

Here is a quiz to begin the chapter: what is a desert? A dry, hot place with sand dunes and camels and palm trees and rattlesnakes? Yes . . . and no. Would you believe that the largest desert on earth is Antarctica? The second largest is the Arctic Ice Cap. The only answer above that applies to all the deserts on earth is DRY.

The following characteristics define deserts around the world:

1. All deserts receive, on average, less than ten inches of precipitation per year. Deserts by their nature are highly variable environments. One summer in New Mexico, we received 16 inches of rainfall, and one winter the temperature dropped to 17 degrees below zero. Such low rainfall makes deserts exceedingly dry or arid places requiring extraordinary adaptations by plants and animals. The polar ice caps may be covered with ice but they are actually very dry places that receive very little new snow.

2. Deserts have very high rates of water loss from evaporation and transpiration, which is the evaporation of water from plant leaves. In summer, early morning humidity can be 40% and by 2:00 pm may be as low as 10%.

3. Deserts have uneven and unpredictable rain and even, occasionally, snow.

4. Deserts often lack sufficient vegetation to buffer temperature. Intense sunlight makes the ground very hot during the day. Night time temperatures fall quickly, often to near freezing or below, because there are no plants to hold the ground heat.

5. When the desert soil reaches high temperatures (120 degrees) the air above is also very hot and rises quickly. Rising air creates a low pressure area and all that air movement makes a desert a very windy place.

6. Deserts are found at varying elevations. Parts of the Mojave Desert are below sea level, the Chihuahuan Desert averages 3500 feet above sea level, and the Atacama Desert in Chile is 7000 feet above sea level. The common characteristic is clear air which allows intense sunlight, often up to 90%, to reach the ground, with ultraviolet levels at the top of the chart.

7. Desert soil tends to be very dry and sandy and also very alkaline. The alkalinity is often seen as snow-like mineral deposits on the soil surface. These deposits are usually calcium, magnesium and sodium. These minerals accumulate because there is not sufficient rainfall to wash them away. I remember every television western I ever watched as a boy: the cattle or the cowboys or the soldiers would be dying of thirst and smell water, and then our hero would have to prevent them from drinking because the water was contaminated with minerals.

8. Most deserts on earth (except for the Polar Deserts) are located between 23 and 34 degrees North latitude and 23 and 34 degrees South latitude. These areas are referred to as the Horse Latitudes or the Doldrums or the Belt of Calms. The complicated flow of wind and ocean currents create these areas where there is often no wind or strong downdrafts. The Horse Latitudes are important for understanding deserts because the winds in that belt are returning to earth from high altitudes and are dry and cold. When they reach the earth they have a tremendous drying effect on the land that they pass over.

The Chihuahuan Desert

The Chihuahuan Desert is a big place and Bosque del Apache in central New Mexico lies at the northernmost edge of it. The desert reaches almost 1000 miles south to San Luis Potosi in Mexico. The Chihuahuan borders the Sonoran Desert on the west in Arizona and stretches across west Texas all the way to Big Bend National Park. In all, it covers 175,000 square miles, making it the largest desert in North America. It has an average elevation of 3500 feet and receives the bulk of its eight inches of yearly moisture in the form of rain in the annual monsoons of July and August. The Chihuahuan Desert is thought to be one of the most biologically diverse arid regions in the world. Of the approximately 1400 cactus species found in the Americas, almost 450 are found in the Chihuahuan Desert. But those cactus and all that empty space are fragile and at risk.

Visitors to the Chihuahuan Desert probably look at the vast, remote, inhospitable and largely uninhabited Chihuahuan Desert and wonder what could possibly be a threat to this environment? The threats are real, both historic and present, and include livestock grazing, water use and plant collecting. The Chihuahuan Desert, in the 19th century and earlier, had extensive grasslands even in west Texas and the Big Bend area. Grasslands? In the desert?

The grasses of the desert are warm season grasses and typically don't even germinate until the rains of summer arrive. One species in particular, giant sacaton, stands up to six feet tall and forms clumps three feet in diameter. Spanish, and later American, settlers and ranchers believed that there was so much grass for their cattle that it would never be exhausted. By 1900, the desert grasslands of west Texas were home to over nine million cattle. The 19th century was cooler and wetter than normal and when the climate changed in the 20th century, cattle herds declined by 70%. However, the damage was already done and continues due to overgrazing which destroys the native grass and allows shrubs such as saltbush, creosote, cholla, sagebrush and mesquite to become dominant.

Global climate change is really just a continuation of a drying trend that began in the Southwest centuries ago. As the water has disappeared, population growth and agriculture have stretched the water resources to their limits. Surface water is easier to exploit and has been fully allocated but isn't enough. Ground water sources are now being mined to meet society's needs.

Cactus collecting has devastated populations in the Chihuahuan Desert because many of the species are found only in small areas, a single arroyo or mountainside. Both the United States and Mexico recognize the problem and have made efforts to prevent cactus smuggling but the volume of traffic, for example between El Paso, Texas, and Juarez, Mexico, makes inspection difficult. However, a new generation of cactus collectors is having a positive effect. These collectors venture into the desert to collect seed, not plants. They propagate the seed and sell the plants to collectors, landscapers and nurseries.

A view of the Chihuahuan Desert at Bosque del Apache

Just the Desert Facts, Ma'am!

Top Eleven Largest Deserts (remember: less than 10 inches precipitation)
1.   Antarctica Desert   5,500,000 sq. mi.
2.   Arctic Desert   5,400,000 sq. mi.
3.   Sahara   3,300,000 sq. mi.
4.   Arabian   900,000 sq. mi.
5.   Gobi   500,000 sq. mi.
6.   Kalahari   360,000 sq. mi.
7.   Great Victoria   220,000 sq. mi.
8.   Patagonian   200,000 sq. mi.
9.   Syrian   200,000 sq. mi.
10.   Great Basin   190,000 sq. mi.
11.   Chihuahuan   175,000 sq. mi.

Deserts cover 1/3 of the land surface of the earth, and 20% of them are sand.

Thirty million acres are turned into desert every year.

The Sonoran Desert supports as many as 200 rattlesnakes per square mile.

Sand from the Sahara blows west and falls into the Amazon providing nutrients for the rainforest.

The Atacama Desert in northern Chile is the driest place on earth. Since record keeping began, parts of the Atacama have never had rain.

Camels once roamed the deserts of Arizona.

Alaska has a sand desert with dunes 150 feet high.

In six hours, the world's deserts receive more solar energy than humans use in a year.

Christmas and Easter cactus and epiphylum are true cacti, but they grow in the hot wet jungles of Mexico and Central and South America.

Cacti are only native to North, Central and South America. There are plants found in South Africa, Madagascar and Australia that resemble cactus but belong to euphorbia and other plant families.

What is a Cactus?

What do a cactus and an apple tree have in common? Everything!

Okay, it's a trick question, because they don't seem alike at all. They both have flowers, fruit, leaves, stems, roots and trunks, but a cactus is a highly specialized and adapted plant that grows in the driest regions on earth. Let's consider a few of the adaptations.

Cacti are able to store water in their bodies. This comes in handy when precipitation in the desert is less than ten inches and the humidity is often under ten percent. Many cacti resemble accordions. The stem will swell and shrink as the plant takes in moisture and reluctantly gives it up. A mature saguaro cactus in the Sonoran Desert can absorb up to 200 gallons of rainwater. Most cacti tend to be short and fat, which maximizes volume and minimizes surface area.

Rainfall in the desert often comes in small amounts and doesn't soak very deeply into the soil. Cacti take advantage of this by having extensive but shallow roots. The roots actually can change character in response to rainfall. The plant can grow new rain roots to absorb additional moisture and then shed those roots if dry times resume.

Cactus spines are actually highly modified leaves that no longer contain chlorophyll for energy production. Chlorophyll is found in the cactus body. No leaves also means far less water loss. Spines also protect the plant from predators and provide some shade from the intense desert sun.

Cacti are very careful about water loss. During dry times the only water they have available may be what they can store in their own cells. A cactus develops a very tough waxy outer skin that is impervious to water loss. A typical plant "breathes" during daylight hours by transpiration. This is when the plant opens the tiny pores in its leaves, called stomata, in order to exchange oxygen and carbon dioxide. In a humid environment, the loss of water by the plant will be minimal. In the desert, loss of water can be fatal. Cacti solve this problem by opening their stomata at night when the temperature is lower and the desert humidity is higher and so less water is lost. Unlike other vascular plants, cactus stomata are located on the stem or the fleshy fat trunk. This is a very effective strategy for a cactus, but the result is much lower efficiency of photosynthesis, and thus much slower growth. This is the strategy used by most desert plants, and it seems like a fair trade: slow growth in order to have a long life.

When you observe a cactus, notice the white fuzzy spots on the stem. These are called areoles and are completely unique to cactus. Remember that cactus have all the usual plant parts (roots, stems, leaves, flowers, fruits, seeds). Areoles are modified branches that are highly specialized. All of the functions of the various cells on a branch of a typical plant are packed into that little fuzzy spot. The areole is the base of the spines, and new spines grow from there as well as flowers.

Cacti and all the plants of the world's deserts are very highly adapted to their environments. They are very successful, but they are also very vulnerable. All cacti are at risk according to the Convention on International Trade in Endangered Species (CITES). The greatest threats come from development, over-grazing and over-collection. Housing developments, dams and highways, unless done carefully, can wipe out entire species that may exist in one canyon or hillside. Grazing often reduces the natural diversity of the plant community and creates a monoculture such as sagebrush. CITES now discourages illegal collecting and sale but hasn't stopped it. Many cactus lovers have seen a business opportunity and now collect seed from wild cactus and grow cactus for sale to collectors, landscapers and nurseries.

The new and emerging threat is climate change. The deserts of the world are likely to become hotter and drier with more unpredictable weather. Time will tell how our slow-growing cactus will respond to rapid change.

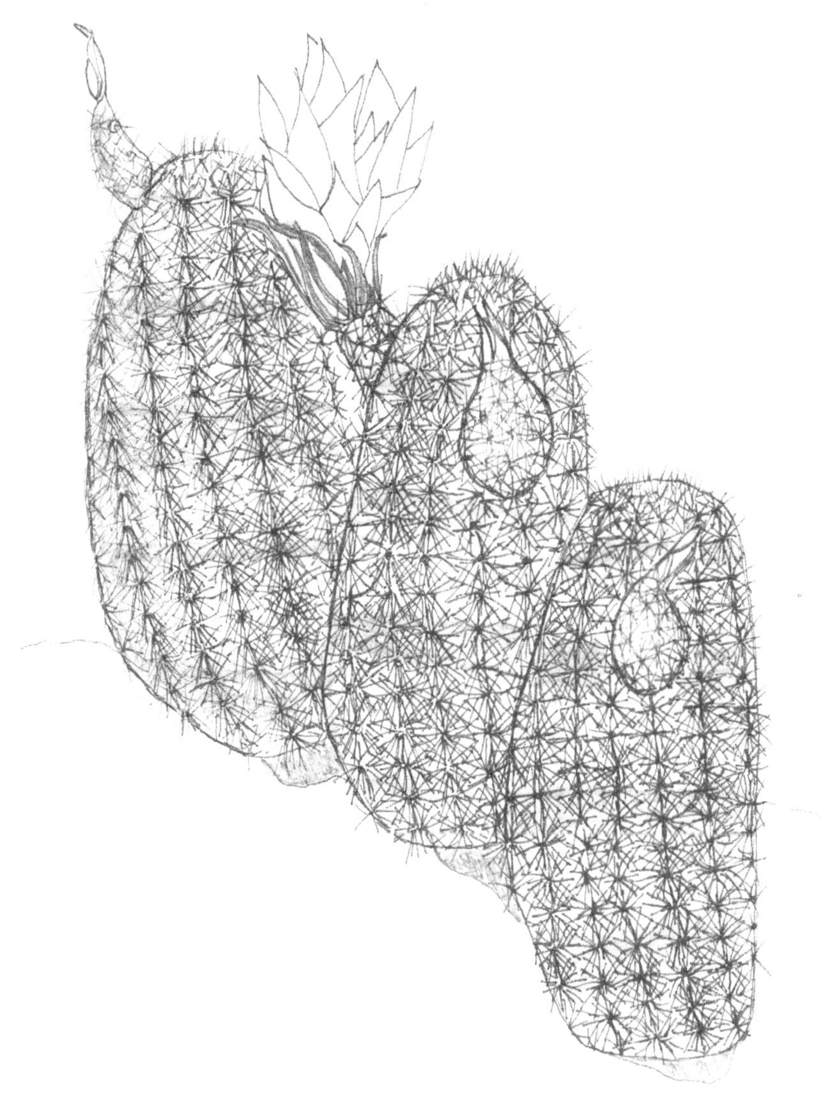

Echinocereus dasyacantha

The Botanists

Finding a new species is a cause for celebration among botanists and biologists. Naming a new species is something of a sacred rite and an art form taken very seriously among scientists. Rarely do researchers name plants after themselves but rather choose to honor an esteemed colleague, mentor, local geographical feature near the discovery or something unique about the structure or appearance of the plant.

The 18th and 19th centuries were a golden age for botany. Many young and ambitious botanists, often from Columbia and Harvard Universities, were tramping through jungles and deserts to record the diversity of the natural world. The Desert Arboretum at Bosque del Apache is a kind of record of these young men's adventures. At least 27 species of plants in the collection bear the name of some prominent botanist of that time. One stimulus for research was the end of the Mexican-American War (1846-1848) and the opening of the southwestern US to exploration and settlement. What follows are the names of the botanists, soldiers and engineers honored by being part of a plant name. Note the number of German botanists on the list. I also include the plant that is named for each botanist.

Frances Bonker (1904-1981) Botanist and writer specializing in cacti, and the only woman on the list. [Bonker's pinkflower hedgehog cactus](*Echinocereus bonkerae*)

Estaban (1776-1813) and Claudio (1774-1842) Boutelou These Spanish botanists were brothers. Blue grama (*Bouteloua gracilis*), sideoats grama (*Bouteloua curtipendula*) and black grama (*Bouteloua eriopoda*) are all named after them.

William Boyce-Thompson (1869-1930) American mining engineer who made a fortune on Arizona copper. His ranch east of Phoenix became the Boyce-Thompson Arboretum State Park. [Boyce-Thompson hedgehog cactus] (*Echinocereus boyce-thompsonii*)

John Brickell (1748-1809) Irish-born physician and naturalist. [California Brickellbush](*Brickellia californica*)

Frederick Coville (1867-1937) American botanist on the Death Valley Expedition 1890-1891. Worked as chief botanist for the USDA and as first director of the United States National Arboretum. [Sonoran barrel] (*Ferocactus covillei*)

George Engelmann (1809-1884) German-American botanist who specialized in the plants of the western US. [Engelmann prickly pear](*Opuntia engelmannii*)

Charles Faxon (1846-1918) American botanist and instructor of botany. [Faxon's yucca](*Yucca faxoniana*)

August Fendler (1813-1883) A Prussian-born botanist who studied New Mexico plants as a favor to Asa Gray. [Fendler's hedgehog cactus](*Echinocereus fendleri*)

James Duncan Graham (1799-1851) Topographical engineer and surveyor with US-Mexico Border survey. [Graham's nipple cactus](*Mammillaria grahamii*)

Asa Gray (1810-1888) The most important botanist in the US in the 19th century. He influenced or taught many of the men on this list.

Josiah Gregg (1806-1850) American merchant, explorer, naturalist and author. He wrote *Commerce of the Prairies* about the American Southwest and has 47 plants named after him. [Night-blooming cereus](*Peniocactus greggii*)

Hermann Gruson (1821-1895) German engineer, inventor and amateur botanist. [Golden barrel](*Echinocactus grusonii*)

Valery Havard (1846-1927) Born in France, he became a US Army physician in the West and studied botany, especially cactus. [Havard's agave](*Agave havardiana*)

Jacob Theodor Klein (1665-1759) German-born historian, botanist, zoologist, mathematician and diplomat who served Polish King August the Strong. [Klein's cholla](*Cylindopuntia kleinae*)

Stepan Krascheninnikov (1711-1755) Russian botanist, explorer and geographer who explored Siberia and the Kamchatka Peninsula. [winterfat](*Krascheninnikovia lanata*)

Gotthilf Muhlenberg (1753-1815) German-American clergyman and botanist. [Bush muhly grass](*Muhlenbergia porteri*)

Charles Parry (1823-1890) British-American botanist and mountaineer. He studied botany at Columbia University under John Torrey, Asa Gray and George Engelmann. He was a member of the US-Mexican Boundary Survey from 1848-1855. [Parry's agave](*Agave parryi*)

Heinrich Gustav Reichenbach (1823-1889) German botanist and expert on orchids. [lace cactus](*Echinocereus reichenbachii*)

Arthur Schott (1814-1875) German-American artist, engineer, geologist and botanist who worked on the US-Mexican Boundary Survey from 1848-1850. [Schott's yucca](*Yucca x schottii*)

John Torrey (1796-1873) American botanist, chemist, and physician. He wrote about the flora of New York, Mexico, US-Mexican Boundary Survey and Pacific Railroad Survey. [Torrey yucca](*Yucca treculeana*)

James Toumey (1865-1932) American botanist who specialized in cactus. He taught at the University of Arizona. [Toumey's agave](*Agave toumeyana*)

Thomas Wheeler (1754-1847) British botanist and apothecary and devotee of Linnaeus. [sotol](*Dasylirion wheeleri*)

Lt. Amiel Whipple, US Army (1818-1863) Engineer and surveyor with the 1853 Pacific Railroad survey. He wrote about western plants and cactus and died at the Battle of Chancellorville in 1863 in the American Civil War. [Whipple's cholla](*Cylindropuutia whipplei*)

Ira Wiggins (1899-1987) American botanist and biologist; graduate of Stanford University, also taught at Stanford. Traveled and studied the Sonoran Desert and Alaska. [Wiggin's cholla](*Cylindropuntia wigginsii*)

Frederick Wislizenus (1810-1889) A German-born American botanist, physician, and explorer who traveled in northern Mexico and New Mexico. [Arizona barrel cactus] (*Ferocactus wislizeni*)

Charles Wright (1811-1885) American botanist with several railroad surveys in the West. He identified dozens of new species of cactus. [Wright's pincushion cactus](*Mammillaria wrightii*)

George Engelmann

Opuntia engelmannii

What's in a name?

Naming the world around us is one way we understand its diversity and complexity. For the names to makes sense, we must agree on using the same name for the same thing. Here is an extreme example of a plant (*Escobaria vivipara*) with more than one common name: Long Mamma, foxtail cactus, big needle cactus, big nipple Cory cactus, nipple beehive cactus, (in Spanish) Dona Ana, Biznaga partida, Donana and (in Tarahumara) Dona-ra.

There is a system in the study of the natural world called binomial nomenclature, otherwise known as *genus* and *species*. This system is meant to eliminate confusion when used to describe exactly which organism one is referring to. Each organism has one, and only one, unique name. The system was created by a Swedish physician named Carl Linnaeus in the 18th century.

Carl Linnaeus was born in Sweden in 1707 and died in 1778. His father was an amateur botanist and Lutheran minister and began at an early age to tutor young Carl in mathematics, Latin and geography. Linnaeus eventually attended grammar school and university where one of his teachers informed his father that his son, despite studying Greek, Hebrew, mathematics and theology, would probably never become a scholar. Linnaeus eventually completed degrees in botany, zoology and medicine. Linnaeus was very much a product of the European Enlightenment along with such contemporaries as Goethe and Rousseau and Thomas Jefferson. The Enlightenment was based on the belief that the power of reason could bring dramatic improvements to society and progress in the human condition. Human autonomy was the goal of the Enlightenment and could be achieved by thinking rationally.

The Enlightenment was also a revolution in scientific thinking and study. Modern medicine, physics and the biological sciences made dramatic advances in the 18th century. Young university graduates in botany and zoology like Linnaeus were traveling the world collecting and cataloging the natural world. In 1732, at age 25, Linnaeus made a trip on foot and on horseback through Lapland in Sweden. It was on this trip that he began to test his ideas about classification of plants and animals.

Linnaeus's first classification system was based on plants' sexual reproduction. He realized that he could categorize plants by the number and position of stamens, pistils, etc. His system also included the use of a hierarchical set of steps that are still in use today as the basis of plant and animal taxonomy: kingdom, phylum, order, genus and species. The category "family" was later added between "order" and "genus" due to the immense number of organisms being discovered. This first attempt at a system was limited by using arbitrary divisions and was not broad enough to classify all the species being discovered. The system that we use today was devised by Linnaeus to use "natural characters" or descriptions of plant structures. It was broad enough to classify all the plants and animals being brought back to university laboratories from trading posts and colonies all over the world.

Linnaeus's most lasting achievement brings us back to binomial nomenclature--*genus* and *species*. This system of naming plants and animals, which he perfected in 1742, is still the backbone of plant and animal sciences. It also reflects the values of 18th century Enlightenment: rational, universal, advancing greater knowledge of the natural world and human progress.

Finally, two questions remain. First, how does the naming process work? To illustrate, I'll use plants found in the Desert Arboretum at Bosque del Apache. You probably found a cactus in the Arboretum called green-flowered hedgehog cactus, also known as New Mexico rainbow cactus. The binomial names are a combination of Greek and Latin words. The binomial name is *Echinocereus viridiflorus*. *Echino* means hedgehog, *cereus* means candle, and *viridiflorus* green-flowered. This cactus grows in clusters of stems. Put together, we have "candles that look like hedgehogs and have green flowers."

Banana yucca grows all over New Mexico, and we have several in the garden. Its botanical name is *Yucca baccata*. The word *Yucca* is a variant of the Carib Indian word for cassava, which Linnaeus confused as being the same. The word *baccata* means "bearing berries" in Latin and refers to the yew tree. The fruit of *Yucca baccata* very much resemble green bananas.

Second, why is the binomial system based on Latin and Greek? Latin and Greek were the languages of the university and the church in the 18th century and in the Middle Ages. University students learned, spoke and wrote both. The Catholic Church used Latin for the mass. Latin and Greek were the languages that scholars could use and find agreement across borders and disciplines and even centuries. Imagine the arguments that would have erupted had the French and Germans and English and Italians all made a case for theirs to be the language of science!

1. Central spines 0–3, stout or relatively stout, when present, with prominent bulbous bases; radial spines 14–23, pectinately arranged, relatively stout, usually laterally compressed at their bases (2).
1. Central spines 6–12, relatively thin and flexible, with smallish-bulbous bases; radial spines 30–45, appressed or spreading, slender, flexible, usually terete at their bases (4).

2(1). Central spines three or more per areole [will also key under second lead 1 above]; lower central spine usually white, mostly white or white on the upper surface, 2.5–4.3 cm long, directed downward but usually curving upward; Culberson Co. W to El Paso Co. and S NM; (in part)

E. viridiflorus var. *chloranthus*, p. 175

2. Central spines 0–3; lower central, when present, colored like the other central spines (yellow, reddish, or reddish-brown, rarely whitish), 0.7–1.4 cm long, directed downward or porrect, straight or slightly curved; mostly Jeff Davis and northern Brewster counties (3).

3(2). Plants all or mostly with a red or red-brown and white aspect; flowers usually unscented, typically opening only about 45°, of any color; radial spines 14–23; a familiar cactus of the Davis Mts and elsewhere

E. viridiflorus var. *cylindricus*, p. 170

3. Plants all with a greenish-yellow and tan or ashy-white aspect; flowers lemon-scented, widely opening, all yellow-green; radial spines 19–28; mostly restricted in the northern Marathon Basin

E. viridiflorus var. *correllii*, p. 172

4(1). Stems clothed in white spines; colored spine tips, when present, all red-purple (no yellow color-form present); seedlings with long, white, hairlike spines and not stiff spines in the areoles; flowers bright, light green; distribution Solitario Dome in SE Presidio Co.

E. viridiflorus var. *canus*, p. 186

4. Not as above; either spines are fewer, or yellow color-forms present, or seedlings normal, or flowers varying to red/brown; distribution not in the Solitario (5).

5(4). Central spines 5–12 or fewer [will also key under first lead 1 above], relatively thin and flexible, acicular, with smallish-bulbous bases; radial spines 30–45, appressed or spreading, slender, flexible, usually terete at the base; (in part when spines are numerous)

E. viridiflorus var. *chloranthus*, p. 175

5. Not as above (6).

From *Cacti of Texas, a Field guide* by Powell, Weedin and Powell, 2008

The Supermarket in the Desert

What's for dinner? Is there anything to eat out here in the desert? I remember watching television westerns when the cowboy dying of thirst would find a barrel cactus and cut it open, eat the watery pulp and save himself. I know people who make jelly from cactus and mesquite fruit. But we can't survive on a diet of jelly and cactus pulp. What else is there?

We know that indigenous people managed quite well, had a varied diet and had a use for almost every plant and animal they found. For this discussion, we'll set aside the obvious food sources, like deer, antelope, fish and pine nuts. They were always intermittent but very rich food sources. Native people were surrounded with food plants even in the desert. Getting food from the plants often required hard labor and the food, although low in calories, was plentiful. Here is a brief look at several desert food plants.

Agave

The best known product made from agave is the alcoholic beverage mescal and its variation, tequila. The agave plant is uprooted, the leaves are trimmed off and the center, or heart, is roasted, fermented and then distilled. Indigenous people also ate the roasted agave heart. The flowers, as well as the leaves, can be eaten in the spring. The leaves store water in a sweet solution, and that liquid can be extracted and boiled to make agave syrup to be used as a sweetener. The leaves are very fibrous and, once those fibers are removed, they can be used for weaving.

Yucca

There are a dozen or so species of yucca growing in the Chihuahuan Desert, and most of them would have been used by native people. The leaves are all fibrous and yield materials for weaving and basket-making. The New Mexico state flower is the soaptree yucca (*Yucca elata*), and its roots are composed of a chemical that acts like soap and is used as shampoo. The fruit can be roasted and eaten or dried and ground into meal and used for baking. The immature flowers and mature seeds are also eaten.

Sotol

Sotol (*Dasylirion wheeleri*) is a yucca relative with a tall flower spike and very sharp saw-edged leaves. The root is used for a northern Mexican version of mescal called sotol. These large "hearts" of yucca, as well as agave and sotol, need to be baked in an earth oven for 36-48 hours. The long process converts the largely inedible long-chain carbohydrates to simple sugars. The leaves are used for weaving once the sharp edges have been peeled away.

Mesquite

Mesquite is a medium-sized native tree of the American Southwest and northern Mexico. There are over 30 species, and we have two in the Bosque del Apache: honey and screwbean. Honey mesquite (*Prosopsis glaundulosa*) makes a seed pod that resembles a garden bean while the screwbean (*Prosopsis pubescens*) pod looks like a wood screw. Mesquite has long been used for food by native people. The pods are picked and dried and the beans discarded because they are far too hard to eat. The pods are then ground to meal and, with a little water, made into patties and baked or fried. The meal can also be used to thicken soup. When the flour is mixed with sufficient water, the mixture will ferment and an alcoholic beverage similar to beer can be made. Mesquite flour is a very healthy ingredient because it is gluten free, and the sugar in the flour is in the form of fructose so it does not require insulin for its digestion.

Prickly Pear

Prickly pear cactus is probably most people's idea of a cactus. It usually has lots of spines, and its flat pads look like leaves and are edible and very tasty. They are a very traditional food in the US Southwest and Mexico. Prickly pears bloom in the spring and make a fruit full of seeds that can be as small as an acorn up to the size of a large plum. In Mexico, the fruit are called "tunas," and they are greatly savored because they are only available in the late summer. They are used to make jams, jellies, cold drinks and salads. The cactus pads, actually highly modified stems, are called "nopales" and are available year round. Nopales are sliced and added to salads or sauted and mixed with scrambled eggs. Both nopales and tunas must be handled carefully because, in most species, they are covered with tiny spines called glochids. The preferred species is a Mexican native called Barbary fig or *Ficus indica*. Neither the tuna nor the pad has spines. This species is grown commercially in Mexico.

Banana yucca (*Yucca baccata*)

Agave havardiana

Agaves and Yuccas

Most people know agaves as "century plants" because they are thought to bloom only once every hundred years. In fact, they can bloom any time if conditions are right, but blooming plants are usually between five and fifty years of age. When the agave decides to bloom, the plant puts all its energy and stored water into the bloom spike which can be up to 20 feet tall. The spike will grow to that height in as little as two weeks, growing six inches a day, after which the individual flowers begin to open. Agave flowers have a very distinctive smell and attract a host of pollinators including bees, wasps, hummingbirds, orioles and bats. By the time the flowers have opened and are being pollinated, the agave plant is beginning to die. Agaves don't depend exclusively on pollination of their flowers for reproduction. Most species hedge their bets by sending out underground roots that pop up new little plants (pups) around the parent plant.

Many agaves depend on bats for pollination, and this has become a very tenuous relationship. Long-nosed bats travel several thousand miles from central Mexico to southeast Arizona to their nesting roosts. They depend on at least 16 different species of agaves being in bloom to provide food for the trip. The world-wide popularity of tequila, which is a product of Mexico, has led to commercial cultivation of agave, but it has also led to increased harvesting of wild agave, both for commercial sale and private use. The traditional species used for tequila is blue agave, but all species are being harvested. The commercialization of agave to produce tequila has dramatically reduced the wild agave and so further endangered migratory bat populations.

Humans have had a long relationship with agave. Every part of the plant has a use. The sharp tips of the leaves can be used as sewing needles, the leaves themselves for fiber and even for roof shingles. The juice from the leaves is made into agave nectar, which is similar to maple syrup. The heart of the plant can be roasted and eaten or ground into a pulp which is then fermented and distilled and becomes mescal and tequila. The sweet pulp from the heart is also used in northern Mexico to make an alcoholic beverage called *pulque*.

Yuccas are closely related to agaves and, along with sotol and nolina, are members of the asparagus family, their flower spikes closely resembling an asparagus sprout. Yuccas are native to Central and North America and are found from Guatemala through Mexico and the Baja Peninsula across the western US to Alberta, Canada, and as far east as Virginia. Yuccas bloom every year and survive the process (as opposed to agaves). There are 49 species of yucca found in the Americas and at least several of them depend on the yucca moth for pollination. The moth carries pollen from one plant to another achieving necessary cross-pollination, but it also lays eggs on the flower. The larvae eat the resulting seeds but manage not to eat all of them.

Yuccas provide many of the same products as agave. The root can be processed and used to make an alcoholic beverage. The seed pods can be eaten green or baked and eaten. The flowers are also edible. The roots of yuccas and many other desert plants can be made into soap, and fibers from the leaves and stalks can be used to make cloth, rope, sandals and baskets.

Fourwing Saltbush *(Atriplex canescen)*

Fourwing saltbush is a three-to-eight-foot tall perennial evergreen shrub that can be found throughout the entire western US from the Mississippi River to the Pacific Ocean, and Canada to Mexico. The name comes from the four papery wings that grow on the seed pod. The plant has small fuzzy leaves and is very dense and heavily branched. Many desert birds and animals eat the seeds. In Bosque del Apache, fourwing saltbush is found where the arroyos (dry creeks) empty into the river valley and on up in elevation to about 6000 feet.

Fourwing saltbush was a very important plant for the Native American people living in the Southwest. It was critical in the process of making corn palatable and nutritious. The native people of the Southwest were largely settled farmers, and they relied on corn, beans, squash, wild plants and wild game for survival. The Zuni, Hopi, Pueblo and many other tribes were very successful at growing corn. The Hopi were thought to have grown up to 30 different varieties of corn, each variety matched to a specific soil type and area. But there are two problems with a corn-based diet: corn has a very hard pericarp, or seed covering, that must be removed for further processing, and corn is deficient in niacin. The solution is to soak the corn in water with slaked lime to soften and remove the seed coat. In the absence of slaked lime, the Southwest tribes found that the ashes from burned sticks of fourwing saltbush had the same effect. Saltbush is also rich in niacin, which soaked into the corn kernels and prevented the native people from contracting pellagra, a niacin deficiency disease.

This is an example of one of the most fascinating aspects of studying native food and medicine. How did early humans discover what was good for them and what might kill them? They must have tried many variations and been sensitive and intuitive enough to see, smell and taste the successful combinations.

But back to corn. The process of soaking and boiling corn for further use is nixtamalization, an Aztec word. The benefits are immense, for without nixtamalization, corn meal will not make dough, and the taste and aroma of the corn are improved. There are also often toxins present in corn that are almost entirely removed by the process. The rubbery seed coat can also be removed after soaking.

The process has these steps:

1.   remove whole, dried corn kernels from cob

2.   add slaked lime or ashes, and water

3.   boil

4. steep

5. wash

6. grind

The ground corn is now masa, which can be used as fresh dough or dried for flour.

Fourwing saltbush has become an important management tool to fight desert encroachment. Plantings can be used to stabilize moving sand dunes and to re-habilitate mine spoils and roadsides and to re-vegetate saline sites. Every living organism needs salt but only in very small quantities. Saltbush grows in a very sodium-rich environment and deals with the excessive sodium by depositing it in bladders on its leaves, keeping it away from the living cells. The salt on the leaves falls to the ground, but is also attractive to animals that lick it off or eat the leaves, either way removing it from the plant. The extra salt on the leaves can even attract water from the air which the plant can absorb.

Fourwing saltbush

Endangered Plants: Three Short Stories

Golden barrel cactus

The golden barrel cactus *(Echinocactus grusonii)* is a very popular landscape plant around the world. There are spectacular displays of golden barrels in several botanical gardens, especially the Huntington Botanical Garden in Los Angeles and the Boyce-Thompson Arboretum in Phoenix. The golden barrel was discovered and named in 1889 and immediately became a sensation as thousands were dug up and shipped all over North America and Europe for collectors and botanical gardens. By 1900, botanists were expressing concern about the survival of golden barrel in the wild. The cactus only grows in two areas, one in Queretaro State and the other in Hidalgo State, both in Mexico. The most recent threat came in 1993 when the World Bank-financed Zimapan Dam was completed in central Mexico. The dam flooded the Rio Moctezuma Valley, one of the last remaining habitats of the cactus, with one million acre-feet of water and a reservoir of nine square miles. Fortunately, the golden barrel has survived, just not in its native habitat.

Giant pincushion cactus

The giant pincushion cactus is on the US Endangered Species List and is protected in Arizona, its native habitat. We get into a bit of a taxonomic muddle here as this cactus is known both as *Coryphantha sheeri* and *Coryphantha robustispina.* It has about a dozen common names. Sprawling development in southern Arizona has threatened the habitat of the giant pincushion cactus, but there is another threat that involves the complicated life cycle of this little plant. The cactus blooms during the summer rains, and the short-lived flowers must be pollinated by one particular species of bee. Pollinated flowers then develop into a seed pod which can be eaten by various desert animals. The pod must be eaten by a jackrabbit, not a cottontail because the cottontail's teeth are different and will grind up the seed. The lucky seed then passes through the jackrabbit and is deposited in rabbit scat. The scat protects the seed until one particular species of termite finds the seed and chews on it and, combined with the summer rain, the seed can now germinate. If any of these steps are missed, reproduction fails. Fortunately, the seeds collected by cactus growers germinate readily in greenhouses and can grow into mature plants.

Santa Fe cholla

Santa Fe, New Mexico, has seen 40 years of steady home and strip mall construction. In 2002, two Santa Fe cactus collectors discovered that a rare species of cactus, Santa Fe cholla *(Opuntia viridiflorus)*, was being threatened. The builders were apparently bulldozing the chollas because they looked similar to the very common tree cholla. Luckily, there were a few plants protected in a nearby park and a few more growing near Pojoaque village. The two plant collectors realized that, not only did they have a new species, but they had one that was at risk and that they could do something to save it. The botanical parks in Albuquerque and Santa Fe began propagating cuttings and donating them to other parks and gardens. Now the lucky little chollas are spread all over northern New Mexico.

One other item of interest: the Santa Fe cholla appears to be a natural cross between tree cholla (*Cylindropuntia imbricata*) and Whipple's cholla (*Cylindropuntia whipplei*), both native New Mexican species.

Golden barrel cactus *(Echinocactus grusonii)*

Larrea tridentata

Creosote Bush (*Larrea tridentata*)

Creosote bush is the dominant plant of the American Southwest and Northern Mexico and is found in the Chihuahuan, Sonoran and Mojave deserts. As the reader drives to and from Bosque del Apache, the olive-green shrubs seen growing in the desert are all creosote.

Creosote bush is a medium-sized shrub standing three-to-four feet tall in the Chihuahuan Desert and about twice that in the Sonoran Desert, probably due to the Sonoran's milder winters and summer and winter precipitation. There are between 35 and 46 million acres of creosote in the Southwest. Creosote bush survives because of its incredible adaptations to the harsh environments where it grows. The average yearly precipitation in the northern Chihuahuan Desert is eight inches, and average summer humidity is usually 10-12 percent or lower. In the desert southwest, a dry spell is three months without rain, and a drought is six months to two years. One of creosote's adaptations is tiny stiff waxy leaves that reduce evaporation, discourage insects and cattle foraging and protect the leaves from heat and excessive ultra-violet radiation. Another adaptation is related to the smell of creosote bush. The plant produces many oils in its leaves that make it unpalatable to animals. Odors are carried in water vapor in the air. In the dry desert environment there are few smells until the rain comes and then the creosote bush produces a banquet of pine, citrus, tar, camphor and menthol scents.

Creosote bushes are extremely long-lived, often 100 to 200 years. They grow very slowly and, in dry periods, will not grow at all. Seed production is profuse but seed survival is poor. Most creosote bushes reproduce by growing offsets, or clones, of themselves. There is a creosote bush in the Mojave Desert named "King Klone" that botanists have determined is 11,700 years old. It began as a single plant and over time reproduced by clones, slowly forming a circle around the "mother plant." Centuries passed and the circle grew larger and larger until today the ring is 67 feet by 45 feet. Genetically it is regarded as one single organism.

Another striking feature of creosote bush is the spacing between plants. At first glance the plants appear to be planted by someone using a measuring stick. In fact, the plants space themselves and botanists are not certain why. This is a recurring theme in the study of life in the desert: a lack of information and research about how deserts work. At one time it was believed that creosote bushes space themselves by exuding a chemical from the roots that inhibits the growth of other plants. This is a known phenomenon for plant species, but is not known to be true for creosote. More recently it was thought that because creosote, like other desert plants, has a shallow and very finely branched root system which is extremely efficient at water collection, no water is left for other plants. It is possible that both of these ideas may be true.

However, a creosote bush very often provides shelter for other desert plants, usually prickly pear cactus. Imagine that a nearby prickly pear blooms and produces a fruit that is then eaten by a packrat. Later, the packrat, seeking shade, defecates under the creosote. Now the seed has shade and fertilizer and once the rains come, it can germinate protected from the intense heat of the sun.

Creosote bush is one of the native species that moves into degraded and overgrazed grasslands. Cattle won't usually eat it, but jackrabbits, packrats and other rodents eat the seeds and the growing tips. Rodents, mammals, lizards and snakes take cover from the sun in its shade and often find refuge in burrows amongst its roots.

Chamisa *(Ericameria nauseosus)*

Chamisa, also known as rubber rabbitbrush (*Ericameria nauseosus*), is a native to the Chihuahuan Desert but also grows throughout the American West, western Canada and northern Mexico. The rubber in its name comes from the rubbery texture of the dried sap. Native people used the sap for chewing gum and to make tea and cough syrup. The US War Department was interested in rubber rabbitbrush during WWII as a possible alternative to rubber which was scarce during the war. The plant has also been touted as a potential use for gas production from bio-mass conversion.

Chamisa likes dry areas such as arroyos but can be found growing up to 8000 feet elevation. It has marginal value for wildlife because of its strong taste and odor. However, the taste and smell are milder in the winter when deer, rabbits, antelope and birds consume it.

Until recently, chamisa had the binomial of *Chrysothamnus nauseosus*. As often happens in biology, the name has been changed. Now it is *Ericameria nauseosus*. This brings up a topic that is often enlightening but just as frequently annoying (for both botanists and bird watchers!): lumping, splitting and name changing. The process really has the goal of better describing the natural world and fitting plants and animals into cubbyholes with their closest kin. Taxonomists who study desert plants decided that, based on the current information available, chamisa belonged in genus *Ericameria* rather than *Chrysothamnus*. The change is good for science, but also means that we have to learn dozens of new names every few years.

Lumping and splitting are what happens when taxonomists and scholars of ornithology and botany struggle to make relevant and informative categories out of confusing data. Lumpers make categories broadly and assume that differences are not as important as obvious similarities. In the family Cactaceae, lumpers recognize 30-50 genera and 1000 species while splitters see 200 genera and 2000 species. Birdwatchers, at least, can rely on the American Ornithological Union to referee disputes over species, while cactus people have at least four different authorities who all look at the nomenclature slightly differently. For example, in 1969, Lyman Benson, cactus expert and author of *The Cactus of the United States and Canada* decided that, based on his observation, the *Coryphantha* group of cacti had become separated from genus *Mammillaria*. He's usually a splitter, but this time he lumped genus *Escobaria* into *Coryphantha*. In 1970, Benson's colleague Del Weniger, based on Benson's previous work, lumped *Coryphantha* into *Mammillaria*--but only in Texas!

In the cactus garden at Bosque del Apache, we have a little cactus now known as *Escobaria vivipara*. It has several common names , such as spiny star and pincushion cactus, and is also known by its synonyms, *Coryphantha vivipara* and *Mammillaria vivipara*. As if that is not confusing enough, spiny star has six varieties or sub-species. Cactus taxonomy is not for the faint of heart!

Ericameria nauseosa

Prosopis pubescens

Mesquite

There are two species of mesquite growing at Bosque del Apache and in the Desert Arboretum: screwbean mesquite and honey mesquite. Both are small trees, ten- to twenty-feet tall, but with sufficient water, they can grow larger. However, in the Southwest, they occupy two very different niches. Honey mesquite (*Prosopis glandulosa*) grows almost everywhere and anywhere. In the dry desert uplands, it seems to thrive on very little moisture. In Texas, this mesquite is considered a weed species even though it is native. Thousands of square miles of range land have been rendered nearly unusable by solid stands of honey mesquite. It is very invasive, and there are two theories that might explain why. The pods are very attractive forage for livestock, and the animals help carry the seeds wherever they roam. Also, fire suppression in the western US grasslands has allowed mesquite and other trees and woody shrubs to proliferate.

Screwbean mesquite (*Prosopis pubescens*), on the other hand, needs more moisture and so grows in wet soils along the Rio Grande. Screwbean mesquite was once far more widespread than today. The valley of the Rio Grande and other rivers in the Chihuahuan Desert make the best farm land, and sub-developments have displaced the plant. Screwbean mesquite is called *tornillo* (little screw) in Spanish, and if you find a seed pod you will see why.

Susan Tweit, in her beautiful book *Seasons in the Desert* tells a story of Quetzalcoatl, the Aztec god of wind and rain. Quetzalcoatl appeared in human form and taught the Aztec people how to build with stone, how to weave and how to make pottery. He also wanted the people to stop human sacrifice and when they refused, he grew angry and made the land arid and changed their cacao trees into mesquite. He then sailed away, never to return.

Mesquite is another plant of the desert that was used extensively by native people. It makes a strong and durable (and very expensive) building material. The honey mesquite pods were harvested and dried and then ground into a meal called *pinole* and used for baking. Mesquite meal is loaded with minerals and, more importantly, natural sugars and fiber, which make it very good for preventing diabetes.

Ocotillo (*Fouquieria splendens*)

Ocotillo *(Fouquieria splendens)*

Ocotillo is a very strange plant. Most of the year, it looks like a collection of dead spiny sticks waiting for rain. But when the rain comes, ocotillo transforms itself quite suddenly by growing leaves and flowers. Creosote follows a similar but almost opposite strategy by waiting for the rain to flower but keeping its leaves year round. Ocotillo drops its leaves during dry spells but continues to photosynthesize because the bark on the stems is green and contains chlorophyll. Within 12 hours of sufficient rain, tiny leaf buds begin to grow on the barren stems and after 24 hours the stems look fuzzy green with little leaves. If the moisture persists in the soil, ocotillo will make bright red tubular flowers that attract hummingbirds, wasps, orioles and bees. Like so many desert plants, ocotillo must take advantage of rain when it comes. The transpiration rate of ocotillo is normally very low, around 14 milligrams of water per hour which is approximately 0.3 drops of water. Five days after a rain the rate will increase to almost 1900 mg per hour, 0.4 teaspoons or about 40 drops. Ten days later, the ocotillo will drop its leaves and resume life as a dead-looking spiny stick awaiting the next rain.

Ocotillo has many common names: coachwhip, candlewood, slimwood, desert coral, Jacob's staff, Jacob's cactus, vine cactus and flaming sword. It is a member of the genus *Fouquieria*, which also contains the boojum tree. The genus was named after Pierre Fouquier (1776-1850) who was a French physician and doctor to King Charles X.

The Chihuahuan Desert of central New Mexico is the northern limit for ocotillo. It likes rocky, very dry, south-facing slopes in the area east of Bosque del Apache known as the Quebradas. Plants grow from six to fifteen stalks anywhere from five- to twenty-feet tall. The beautiful red flowers are edible. Tohono O'odham women rubbed the flowers on their cheeks for rouge. Ocotillo stems make good walking sticks and are popular fencing material. If conditions are right when the fence is built, the sticks may germinate and produce a living, very spiny fence.

Coyote Melon (*Curcurbita foetidissima*)

Coyote melon is a real melon that grows in the desert. Its binomial is *Curcurbita foetidissima*, which literally means stinking melon. *Curcurbita* is the genus for squash, pumpkins, melons and cucumbers. Coyote melon is well adapted to the desert and needs only minimal water because of the tap root that each plant produces. One spring I attempted to transplant an established coyote melon because it was growing too close to a picnic area. I thought that the plant had a tuber perhaps the size of a sweet potato. I began to dig and uncovered the top of the tuber that was about eight inches in diameter. I kept digging until I reached 18 inches deep and realized that the tuber was at least three feet long and the diameter of my leg. It had also produced lateral branches the size of my arms. It certainly weighed 100 pounds. I gave up, covered up the tuber, and the picnic area was moved.

Coyote melon is another plant with many common names, probably due to its wide distribution: buffalo gourd, stinking melon, Missouri gourd, calabazilla and chilicote, to name a few. Coyote melon is found from California to Missouri and from southern Utah and Colorado to central Mexico. The flowers appear in late spring and are edible. The fruit or melon appears soon after, and in central New Mexico grows to baseball size. What one first notices about the plant is the smell, and it's enough to drive away most foragers. If one was very determined or very hungry, the young melons are edible but bitter. The seeds, later in the summer, can be boiled or roasted for eating. The root, which grows up to 200 pounds, can be dried for flour or meal or pressed for oil, and is high in carbohydrates and protein. The root contains saponin, which can be made into soap. There is some interest in producing biofuels from the carbohydrates in the taproot.

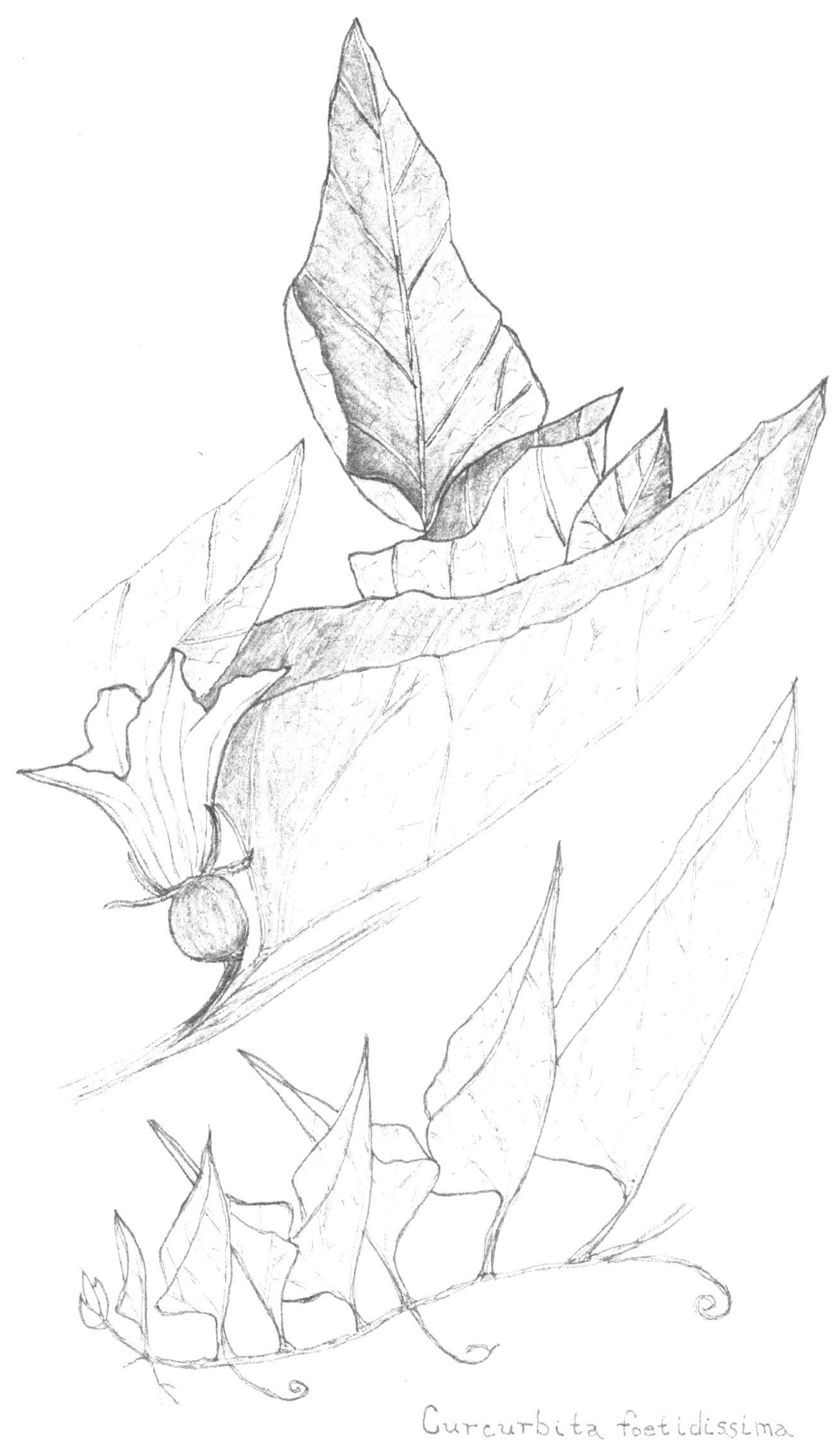

Curcurbita foetidissima

Conclusion

The desert is a place of contrasts and contradictions. The Chihuahuan Desert is a vast landscape that makes one feel small and insignificant. We are surrounded by beautiful plants and animals that one cannot, or dare not, get close to because they are prickly and dangerous. A hike in the desert more often resembles an expedition with layers of clothing, water, walking sticks and sturdy boots. But it's a place that grows on a visitor. One can't help but be inspired by the plants and animals that thrive here. Desert plants are masters of adaptation. Many of these stories have been about their adaptations: shallow roots, spines, small leaves, water storage and bitter taste. I think that their adaptations are what make them so interesting. They have created hundreds of different shapes and colors, all with the same two goals in mind: survival and reproduction. We no longer harvest plants from the desert for landscaping, but the wild plants are still threatened. Climate change will likely make all of our deserts hotter and drier.

Thank you for reading these stories and taking time to appreciate this unique environment.

Acknowledgments

Thank you to:

- Percy, Socorro, and Daniel for building such a beautiful garden
- The Friends of Bosque del Apache for your support of our activities
- Bosque del Apache National Wildlife Refuge for your support of the Desert Arboretum
- Lise Spargo for your superb illustrations and all your hard work
- Robyn Harrison for the layout and editing of this book.

References

archive.bio.ed.ac.uk/jdeacon/desertecology/creosote.htm

arizonadailyindependent.com/2013/07/07/mesquite-trees-provide-food-fuel-medicine-and-more/

Benson, Lyman. The Cacti of the United States and Canada. Stanford University Press, Stanford CA (1982)

blueplanetbiomes.org/saltbush.htm

desertusa.com

Dicht, D.F. and Luthy, A.D.Coryphantha: Cacti of Mexico and the Southern USA. Springer Press, Stuttgart, Germany (2003)

en.wikipedia.org/wiki/Carl_Linneaus

en.wikipedia.org/wiki/Nixtamalization

en.wikipedia.org/wiki/Agave

en.wikipedia.org/wiki/Coryphantha_robustispina

en.wikipedia.org/wiki/Desert

en.wikipedia.org/wiki/Echinocactus_grusonii

en.wikipedia.org/wiki/Fouquieria_splendens

en.wikipedia.org/wiki/King_Clone

en.wikipedia.org/wiki/Lumpers_and_splitters

Fischer, Pierre C. 70 Common Cacti of the Southwest. Southwest Parks and Monuments Association, Tucson, AZ (1989)

gardeningknowhow.com/ornamental/foliage/yucca

Harrison, Robyn. *Bosque del Apache: A Brief History*, 2011.

Hoyt, Cathryn A. The Chihuahuan Desert: Diversity at Risk. Endangered Species Bulletin, Chihuahuan Desert Research Institute. (May-June 2002)

jornada.nmsu.edu/blog/7-things-you-didnt-know-about-creosote-bush

mojavedesert.net/plants/creosote

santafebotanicalgarden.org/May-2013/

texasbeyondhistory.net/ethnobot/images/sotol.html

Tweit, Susan. Seasons in the Desert. Chronicle Books, San Francisco, CA (1988)

usbg.gov/plants/golden-barrel-cactus

Wooten, E.O. & Standley, Paul C. Flora of New Mexico. Contributions from the United States National Herbarium, Volume 19, Smithsonian Instituion, Washington D.C. (1915)